True Friends

*There are many people
that we meet in our lives
but only a very few
will make a lasting impression
on our minds and hearts
It is these people that we will
think of often
and who will always remain
important to us
as true friends*

— Susan Polis Schutz

Friends Are Forever

Featuring poems by
Susan Polis Schutz
and Donna Fargo

Blue Mountain Press ®

SPS Studios, Inc., Boulder, Colorado

Library of Congress Catalog Card Number: 00-035245
ISBN: 0-88396-559-3

ACKNOWLEDGMENTS appear on page 64.

The following poems by Susan Polis Schutz have previously appeared in SPS Studios publications: "Knowing that you are always here...," copyright © 1972 by Continental Publications; "There is no need for...," copyright © 1974 by Continental Publications; "A Friend Is Someone Special," "Regardless of whom I meet...," and "You have such a positive outlook...," copyright © 1982 by Stephen Schutz and Susan Polis Schutz; "Thank You for Being My Friend" and "True Friends," copyright © 1983 by Stephen Schutz and Susan Polis Schutz; "Our Friendship" and "You Are a Perfect Friend," copyright © 1984 by Stephen Schutz and Susan Polis Schutz; "Some people will be your friend...," copyright © 1986 by Stephen Schutz and Susan Polis Schutz; "Friends Are Forever," copyright © 1996 by Stephen Schutz and Susan Polis Schutz.

Registered in the U.S. Patent and Trademark Office.
Certain trademarks are used under license.

Manufactured in the United States of America
First Printing: July 2000

 This book is printed on recycled paper.

Library of Congress Cataloging-in-Publication Data

Schutz, Susan Polis.
   Friends are forever / featuring poems by Susan Polis Schutz and Donna Fargo.
      p. cm.
   ISBN 0-88396-559-3 (alk. paper)
   1. Friendship--Poetry. I. Fargo, Donna. II. Title.

PS3569.C556 F75   2000
811'.54--dc21

                                                    00-035245

SPS Studios, Inc.

P.O. Box 4549, Boulder, Colorado 80306

Contents

A Friend Is Someone Special

A friend is someone who is concerned with everything you do ✦ someone to call upon during good and bad times ✦ someone who understands whatever you do ✦ someone who tells you the truth about yourself ✦ someone who knows what you are going through at all times ✦ someone who does not compete with you ✦ someone who is genuinely happy for you when things go well ✦ someone who tries to cheer you up when things don't go well ✦ someone who is an extension of yourself without which you are not complete ✦

— Susan Polis Schutz

The Best Thing About Our Friendship

The best thing about our friendship
is that it gives me hope
when my inspiration is down.
It makes me feel not so all alone,
even when no one else is around.
It soothes my nerves,
nourishes my spirit,
and lets my soul out to play.
It satisfies my mind
and makes me feel that
my dreams will find a way.

There were many times when
I would have been lost and lonely
if you had not been there for me —
in the background, in the foreground,
or wherever I happened to be.
You taught me that there really is
such a thing as friendship
when I had wondered for so long.
You redefined its meaning
and gave it magic like a song.

Thank you for making my life richer
and for believing in me.
Thank you for always being there
and for helping me to see.
Whether I've been right
or I've been wrong,
with you, I don't have to pretend.
I know you'd never judge me;
you'd just say...
"I love you. I'm your friend."

— Donna Fargo

Our Friendship

There are so many things
to do each day
There is so much going on in the world
of great concern
that often we do not stop and think about
what personally is really important
One of the nicest things in my life
is my friendship with you
and even if we don't have a lot of time
to spend with each other
I want you to always know
how much I appreciate you
and our friendship

— Susan Polis Schutz

I'm So Glad I Have You for a Friend

I've been thinking about how much your friendship means to me and how lucky I am to know you. We've always allowed each other to be ourselves. You've never tried to change me, and I've never tried to change you. We've always wanted the best for each other, and we're happy for each other when we reach our respective goals. I'd be lost without you in my life.

As friends, we've called it like it was and like it wasn't. And each of us would probably admit to ourselves, even if not to each other, that we've made our fair share of what seemed to be less-than-perfect moves. We've trudged through some serious stuff, held each other's eyes open through some "unlighted" tunnels, and kept each other steady when we were being bumped around on some rough roads.

We probably know each other's best and not-so-best sides as well as, if not better than, anyone else.

We've kept our sense of humor when the situation at hand wasn't the least bit funny; we've accepted what we had to do, though sometimes it took a while. We've done our share of hurting, changed a little, and messed up "big time," but we always managed to carry on no matter how we felt or how rocky the ride was. We've cheered each other on and felt burdened when one of us was down. And I just wanted you to hear this from me: My world is better with you in it, my life is happier because you share it, and I'm so glad I have you for a friend.

— Donna Fargo

Some people will be your friend
because of whom you know
Some people will be your friend
because of your position
Some people will be your friend
because of the way you look
Some people will be your friend
because of your possessions
But the only real friends
are the people who will be your friends
because they like you for how you are inside
Thank you for being
one of the very few people in my life
who is a real friend

— Susan Polis Schutz

Our Friendship Means So Much to Me

I promise that I'll thank every wishing star that ever shined for bringing your closeness and understanding to me.

I promise that nothing will ever change the amount of appreciation I have for you. I promise that if I ever have news to share, you'll always be first on the call list. I promise — if I ever release a genie from a magic lamp — I'll share my three wishes with you. In the event that never happens, I promise that you're welcome to split any pizza I might have in my possession. (And the same goes for chocolate.)

I promise I will be there to see you through anything that tries to get you down. I promise that I'll be around through it all, I'll support you in your efforts, and I'll believe in you at all times. We'll do whatever it takes, and together we'll chase away the clouds and keep the sun shining in our lives. When you need to be around someone who truly appreciates your crazy sense of humor, I will gladly, happily, and joyfully be that person.

And because you're such a wonderful friend, I will always feel more blessed than words will ever be able to describe. One of my hopes in life is that someday... I'll find a way to thank you for all this.

But until I do, I'll never take the beauty of our friendship for granted, and I'll never stop trying to tell you how much you mean to me.

I promise.

— L. N. Mallory

You Are a Perfect Friend

You have known me
in good and
bad times
You have seen me
when I was happy
and when I was sad
You have listened to me
when what I said was intelligent
and when I talked nonsense

You have been with me
when we had fun
and when we were miserable
You have watched me
laugh
and cry
You have understood me
when I knew what I was doing
and when I made mistakes
Thank you for
believing in me
for supporting me
and for always being ready
to share thoughts together
You are a perfect friend

— Susan Polis Schutz

Friends are very special people who accept
each other with an unconditional caring. They

Recognize each other's talents and faults and
acknowledge them without judgment.

They are *Incapable* of turning away when times
are tough and life's problems seem hard to bear.

Instead, they *Encourage* each other so they can
enjoy the good times and find strength to endure the

bad times. They're *Never* afraid to say what
they feel and can be honest without causing

hurt or pain. They can *Depend* on each other
because they have the kind of trust

that allows them to *Share* the best
and worst of their lives
with laughter and without fear.

You are one of these special people,
and I'm glad you are my friend.

— Andrea L. Hines

I'll be there for you

If you've got secrets you want to tell,
we can talk all day long. If your dreams
get broken somehow, I'll remind you that
you belong. If you need someplace to
hide, you can hold my hand for a while.
If your sky begins to fall, I'll stay with
you 'til you smile. Whenever you need
some space, there's my room — you can
take it. If someone breaks your heart,
together we'll unbreak it. When you feel
sad or empty inside, I'll show you you're
not alone. If you get lost out there, I'll
come and take you home. I'll go with you
somewhere else, when you need to get
away. And when nothing seems to be
going right and you need a friend...

I'll stay.

— Ashley Rice

Thank You!
Thank You!
Thank You!

I could write you a bunch of "thank you's" and never convey my gratitude to you...

Thank you for your generosity, unselfishness, and friendship. Thank you for being so easy to communicate with. The fact that you're always willing to lend a helping hand is such a welcome attitude. You probably think nothing of it because it is your nature to want to help others, but even that attitude is a credit to you, too.

Although I don't believe that kindness goes unrewarded if I ever forget to say "Thank you," I hope you know that your consideration is not something I take for granted.

Your actions encourage me to care more for others and to spread more good will around. Your attitude reminds me to be more generous and considerate of others. You have taught me many lessons about life and friendship. I will always be encouraged by your example.

Thank you for being such a good teacher and for the many things you continue to do for me. I hope each kindness you have given is someday returned to you.

— Donna Fargo

Ours Is a Friendship
like No Other...

Sometimes a person is blessed with meeting someone
Who will touch their life in a way
That no one else has,
In a way that cannot be explained,
For it is a mutual linking of two hearts,
A bonding of friendship like no other.
You know it is something special
Right from the start,
Even if you have only known the person
For a short time.
But in that time, the foundation
Of a true and lasting friendship
Has already been laid.

A true and lasting friendship
Is built on trust and openness
And understanding.
It is not selfish or demanding and does not
Require you to be someone that you are not.

Rather, it is a friendship
That gives unconditionally
And allows the freedom to express yourself
With no expectations to be anyone different.
It is giving and loving and loyal
And welcomes the sharing of both
Good and bad times with each other.
It brings happiness in thinking of
The other person and
Joy in the time that is spent together.
The warm embraces shared
Have a way of saying everything
That cannot be put into words,
Those things that can be spoken
Only from the heart.

I have been blessed with
Such a special person in my life...
Someone in whose confidence I've trusted
And whose friendship and companionship
I've grown to value and treasure.
Thank you for being such a rare individual;
Thank you for our very special friendship.

— Kathleen L. Biela

"Good Friends"

Good friends are hard to find.
Good friends are easy to love.
Good friends are presents that
   last forever and that feel
      like gifts from above.

Good friends are one in a million.
Good friends are stories to share.
Good friends know the path
   to your happiness,
      and they walk with you
         all the way there.

Good friends are lives overlapping.
Good friends are laughter and tears.
Good friends are emotions so deep
   that the trust just keeps growing
      over the years.

Good friends are hard to find.
Good friends are easy to adore.
And when you've found a good friend
   ...you know that you could ask
      for nothing more.

— Collin McCarty

You Have a Friend in Me Forever

There are certain kinds of friends
who can easily discuss all things,
who feel so utterly comfortable
   with each other,
see one another's inner soul,
and keep faith when things
   go wrong.

For friends like these,
the length of time
they've been together
   is unimportant in determining
      how well they
         know one another,
and distance means nothing,
   for true friendship has
      no boundaries.

If we should ever grow apart
in time or distance —
today, tomorrow,
or in the days ahead —
our friendship will still
be embedded
in my mind,
my heart,
and my soul.
Regardless of where you are,
know that you have a friend
in me...
forever.

— M. Maxine Largman

The Friendship Creed

If you can't be everything to somebody, reach out and just be a friend. Do something nice for someone you care about, something unexpected perhaps, something that would be appreciated if the shoe were on the other foot. Some people walk the other way at the first sign of trouble, but a friend will be there through it all. People are grateful for even the smallest offer of kindness and acceptance. You may never be able to make someone's dreams come true; however, you can give something of yourself to a friend: a call, a note, or whatever you decide... that will do. Always do for a friend what you would want a friend to do for you.

You may not ever be able to do something so important as solving somebody's problems, but you can always do something to make a person feel a little better. It doesn't have to be a big deal or cost a lot of money. It can just be something thoughtful and small. Let that someone know that you're there and that you care about what's happening in his life. You can make someone's world a little better, even for a short while; there are times when we all just need a lift. Don't hold back. Life is too short. Don't wait. Someone might need you. If you can't make somebody's whole life better, then brighten a moment, make a day. It could be important.

— Donna Fargo

The Depth of Friendship

"Friend."
Some people take this word for granted.
They use it to describe almost anyone
who touches their lives.
But that's not fair,
for not everyone fits this word.
It is easy to be a pal, a buddy,
a companion, or an acquaintance,
but to be a friend means
so very much more...

To be a friend
means being trusted and trusting.
Honest and dedicated.
Supportive and available.
It means going strong with
your own life's work and plans,
yet reaching out to another when you're needed
(and maybe even when you're not).

To be a friend is to be fun and fair.
Serious and silly.
To make the mundane exciting.
The unexpected acceptable.
To be the silent stronghold without being asked.
To feel happy for someone else's happiness,
and to share the burden of sorrow
    in thought and action.
To be a friend
is to be strong enough to be leaned on
when someone else cannot walk another step
and to look to that other person
    for your own tranquility
when the world has spun you
    out of control.
It is a lot of giving, a lot of taking,
but most of all, a lot of sharing.

The qualifications of being a friend
are too high for the ordinary to reach.
It takes a while to earn the title
and a lifetime to truly know its meaning.
Never take the job lightly or give it away
    too quickly;
it must be cultivated, nurtured, and cared for.
For when you truly find a "friend,"
you are lucky enough to have one for life.

                                        — Laura V. Nicholson

Regardless of
whom I meet
or what I do
or what I have become
it is the friends
I grew up with
that I feel
closest to
and that I have
the most in common with
Though we don't see
each other often
when we do
it is as though
we were always together —
so comfortable
so natural
so honest
I guess old friends
who know where we come from
who know our backgrounds
who know our families
have an understanding
of us
that no new friend
can ever have

— Susan Polis Schutz

You're So Important to Me

There are some people in my life who really make a difference. They're not just there when they need me, but they're there when I need them. You're one of those important people to me.

You have many qualities that set you apart from others, and I hope you never change. You're considerate, and you're as good as your word. If you say you'll do something, I know you'll try. You're thoughtful and sensitive, and you're genuine in your concern, not just with your words but also by your actions.

I place a high value on loyalty, and it is one of your outstanding virtues. I can depend on you to walk beside me no matter how I'm dealing with life's challenges, and you often go out of your way for me. While others may worry about being taken advantage of and miss the good that could be generated by acts of unselfish generosity, you're not afraid to do more than your part.

It's a pleasure to have you in my life. You live your life in a spirit of cooperation with others, and I believe this attitude is very important for building strong relationships. I always feel that you're on my side and want the best for me, as I hope you know that I'm on your side and want the best for you. In case you don't know it by now, you make a positive difference in my life, and you're so important to me.

— Donna Fargo

I Will Never Forget You
or the Times
We Have Shared

The laughter we shared in happy times
   and the tears in sad ones
will all be tucked away
   in my heart
behind a door marked "Memories of You."
On quiet days of remembrance,
I will remove these thoughts
   one by one,
and I will think of you
   with a happy sadness in my soul.
Though miles and months
   may come between us,
you will still be my friend
   and I will be yours —
always eager to hear from you
   and share your life again.

— Melissa Haynes Chaffin

Our Friendship
Looks like
a Forever Thing to Me

I could keep these feelings inside me. I could not take a chance on telling you how I feel, but what if I died tomorrow and hadn't told you what is in my heart and on my mind? I would have cheated myself and you. I would have missed a chance to show love and acceptance to someone very important to me. Would I be sorry? Yes.

So I'm telling it like it is. I'm making a commitment to you. I'm telling you how I feel and how much I care for you and what an important place you have in my heart and in my life. Our friendship looks like a forever thing to me, and I hope it is.

This commitment to being your friend means that I want the best for you. I thank you for being in my life. I hope our friendship enhances your life and happiness. I depend on you in so many ways. If I haven't made it clear to you before, I want you to know that I'm glad you're in my life.

Friendship is about love, sharing, and commitment. It's about wanting the best for each other and giving each other the freedom to be ourselves with one another. It's about trust, forgiveness, understanding, respect, acceptance, encouragement, and thoughtfulness. These are the qualities that make our friendship very special.

In all the time that we've been friends, I have come to the same conclusion time and time again... You're a very important person in my life, and our friendship looks like a forever thing to me.

— Donna Fargo

Promise Me This

Promise me you'll always remember what a
special person you are ◆ Promise me you'll hold
on to your hopes and reach out for your stars ◆
Promise me you'll live with happiness over the
years and over the miles ◆ Promise me that
when you think of me, it will always be with a
smile ◆ Promise me you'll "remember when…"
and you'll always "look forward to…" ◆ Promise
me you'll do the things you have always wanted
to do ◆ Promise me you'll cherish your dreams
as treasures you have kept ◆ Promise me you'll
enjoy life day by day and step by step ◆
Promise me you'll always remember the wishes
I have for you…

For I wish you
a life of love and joy
and all your dreams
come true.

— Collin McCarty

It's All You Are to Me...
That Makes Me Believe
in You

If you're anything like me, sometimes you feel as though you're better at losing than anything else you do

You lose your temper, your focus, your confidence, your courage, and sometimes even your pride

So if you're ever on a losing streak and wonder if someone will be there for you or if you'll just wind up losing them, too

I just hope you know that you won't lose me and I believe in you

I want to be a source of security for you, someone with whom you share your failures and your triumphs, no matter how big or small

You've got my shoulder to lean on if you need it; all you have to do is call

When your self-esteem is low and your confidence, too, no matter where you are or what you're trying to do

I don't think there's anything that could keep me from saying that I believe in you

If life is a game in which we know the rules but we just can't make the grade

If we do our best but it's not enough while others seem to have it made

It isn't just what you do or don't do that makes me feel the way I do

It's the feelings in my soul, it's all you are to me, that makes me believe in you

— Donna Fargo

There is no need for
an outpouring of words
to explain oneself
to a friend
Friends understand each
other's thoughts even
before they are spoken

— Susan Polis Schutz

Knowing that you are always
here to understand and accept
me helps me get along in the
confused world. If every person
could have someone just like
you, the world would become
a peaceful garden.

— Susan Polis Schutz

You're the friend who's been so good to me,
the one I tell my troubles to,
the one who listens carefully
and always understands.

You're the friend I feel closest to.
There have been so many times when
I gave you all my fears and hurts,
and each time you gave back a heart
filled with love and concern,
a shoulder to rest my worries upon,
and a tranquility found nowhere else
    on earth.

You're the friend who means
    so much to me,
the one I'm thinking of right now,
the one who feels like family in my heart.
And more than anything else,
I want you to know that I'm here for you,
just as you've always been for me...

Because you're the best friend I have.

— Barbara J. Hall

These Are the Words I Would Say on a Long Walk with You

I'd love it if I could find the words in my heart... and take them along on a lovely walk with you. I would even let you choose the season and the time of day — as long as you'd promise to stay close to me, and — if I started to falter — give me the encouragement I need to say the things I'd like to say.

I want you to know that I think you are just about as wonderful as anyone could ever be.

I'd find a way to tell you that. At some point along the path, a perfect moment would arrive. I'd take a deep breath, fill my lungs with a little courage, and I would surprise you, I know... because I so often stay on the "safe" side of things with you. I hardly ever talk about the deeper things and the innermost feelings I have. But on this walk, I would gladly open up and I wouldn't be afraid. And somehow I'd find a way to tell you, before our walk was through...

As long as I live, I will consider the closeness we share to be one of the most precious gifts I could ever receive.

— L. N. Mallory

Thank You for Being My Friend

When things are confused
I discuss them with you
until they make sense

When something good happens
you are the first person I tell
so I can share my happiness

When I don't know what to do
  in a situation
I ask your opinion
and weigh it heavily with mine

When I am lonely
I call you
because I never feel
alone with you

When I have a problem
I ask for your help
because your wiseness helps me to solve it

When I want to have fun
I want to be with you
because we have such a great time together

When I want to talk to someone
I always talk to you
because you understand me

When I want the truth about something
I call you
because you are so honest

It is so essential
to have you in my life
Thank you for being my friend

— Susan Polis Schutz

Friendship

It's like a cool drink of water when we're thirsty or a hot cup of soup when we're cold.

It's an excuse to play "hooky" and stay out of school; it's a walk in the park for the soul.

It's an umbrella to catch the raindrops of life and the stuff that makes beautiful rainbows.

It's a ladder to help us reach higher when we're trying to reach our goal.

It's a safe place to wait when we're trying to get our act together and we don't know quite what to do.

It's like that favorite, familiar security blanket when we feel all alone and blue.

It's a shoulder to cry on, someone to lean on,
a listening ear to understand.

It's a thoughtful word or something someone
didn't say that turns our doubts into "Maybe
I can."

It's the key to some of our prisons, the voice
of acceptance that cheers us on.

It's another living soul who cares if we live or
die and someone we can depend on.

It's a melody between two people that gives
their lives a lift.

It's a room in the heart reserved for someone
special that makes friendship such a gift.

— Donna Fargo

I'll Always Be There
and I'll Always Care;
I'll Always Be Your Friend

There are a thousand things
I would like to be for you...
but one of the most important
is just being
   the someone
      you can talk to.

There are so many things
   I would like
      to do for you,
and so many things I would like
to say and give and share.

But for today
   I just want you to know
that I promise to be
   your friend for life.

I'll always be there,
   and I'll always care.

— A. Rogers

Because our friendship is one of the greatest blessings of my life, I want to wish you these things...

I wish you joy and satisfaction in everything you do, perfect health, and all you need to make life easier to do the things you want to do. I wish you good friends to call on when you need them, and I wish you love and happiness on this day and forevermore.

May the special memories you hold nourish you and remind you of your beautiful life. May your future be filled with positive experiences and realized dreams. May everyone you come in contact with celebrate your loving heart and indomitable spirit.

You're not just another friend to me.
You're one of a kind, unique, and special.
I appreciate your many virtues, and I want
you to know how important your friendship
is to me.

If I could package up these wishes and
make them all come true, they would
require more space than the world has to
offer and they would be too much for one
heart to hold. If I had my say, whatever
you want and need would be yours from
now on.

May all your dreams come true. May you
have exactly what you want. May every
kindness you've given to others be returned
to you and fill your heart with joy.

— Donna Fargo

You have such a
positive outlook on life
Your words are always encouraging
Your face is lit up with excitement
Your actions are so straightforward
Your inner sense helps you achieve
   so much
When people are around you
they seem to absorb your uplifting
   attitude
When I think about you
I can only think
of happiness
and how lucky I am
to know
you

— Susan Polis Schutz

Friends Are So Very, Very Special

Friends teach us some of life's most important lessons. They teach us about love. They search with us for life's meaning. They think out loud with us and give us their approval and judgment. They help us to have faith. By their example, they teach us about truth and honesty. About living. About confidence and favors. They sense when we're lonely and need acceptance.

Friends make us feel at home. We know where we stand with them and where they stand with us. They let us be ourselves and love us even when we are not the most lovable.

Friends don't abandon us when the going gets tough. They are there with us wherever we are, whenever we need them. They have time for us. They don't forget us, and we don't forget them. They give us the opportunity to find out more about ourselves, so we'll know what to try to change and what to accept. Friends validate us.

Friends are not afraid to take a chance on us, to defend us, to take a stand for us. They are not embarrassed to tell us how much our friendship means to them; they do not care how silly they may sound when they share these feelings with us.

Friends are like special gifts to us that we never discard or outgrow. No one can ever take their place. They are always welcome in the rooms of our heart. Theirs are the memories that never fade.

Friends are special... so very, very special. Thank you for being a special friend to me.

— Donna Fargo

Friends Are Forever

Friends always remember so well
all the things they did together
all the subjects they discussed
all the mistakes they made
all the fun they had

Friends always remember
how their friendship
was such a stabilizing force
during confusing times
in their lives

Friends may have different lifestyles
live in different places
and interact with different people
but no matter how much
their lives may change
their friendship remains the same

I know that throughout my life
wherever I am
I will always
remember so well
and cherish our friendship
as one of the best
I have ever known

— Susan Polis Schutz

ACKNOWLEDGMENTS

The following is a partial list of authors whom the publisher especially wishes to thank for permission to reprint their works.

PrimaDonna Entertainment Corp. for the following by Donna Fargo: "The Best Thing About Our Friendship," copyright © 1996 by PrimaDonna Entertainment Corp.; "I'm So Glad I Have You for a Friend," copyright © 1997 by PrimaDonna Entertainment Corp.; "Thank You! Thank You! Thank You!," copyright © 1998 by PrimaDonna Entertainment Corp.; "Friendship," "Because our friendship is....," and "Friends Are So Very, Very Special," copyright © 1999 by PrimaDonna Entertainment Corp.; "The Friendship Creed," "You're So Important to Me," "Our Friendship Looks like a Forever Thing to Me," and "It's All You Are to Me... That Makes Me Believe in You," copyright © 2000 by PrimaDonna Entertainment Corp. All rights reserved. Reprinted by permission.

Melissa Haynes Chaffin for "I Will Never Forget You or the Times We Have Shared." Copyright © 2000 by Melissa Haynes Chaffin. All rights reserved. Reprinted by permission.

A careful effort has been made to trace the ownership of poems used in this anthology in order to obtain permission to reprint copyrighted materials and give proper credit to the copyright owners. If any error or omission has occurred, it is completely inadvertent, and we would like to make corrections in future editions provided that written notification is made to the publisher:

SPS STUDIOS, INC., P.O. Box 4549, Boulder, Colorado 80306.